One Well

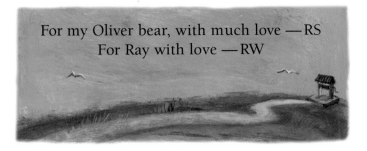

For my Oliver bear, with much love — RS
For Ray with love — RW

ACKNOWLEDGMENTS

I am truly grateful to the many individuals who have made this book possible. My deepest gratitude goes to Valerie Wyatt for her wonderful insights and unfailing guidance and support. Many thanks also to Marie Bartholomew for creating such an inspiring vision and Rosemary Woods for bringing the book to life. Special thanks to Valerie Hussey for patiently allowing me to wade through the content until I found the story. I also want to thank Melissa Clark, Rosanne Metz and my family for eagerly reading drafts and listening to all my watery tales.

Once again, I must praise my incredible team of technical and educational reviewers: Joanne DiCosimo, Mark Graham and Paul Hamilton at the Canadian Museum of Nature; Charles Hopkins, UNESCO Chair and UN University Chair, York University in Toronto, Canada; and Susan Gesner of Gesner and Associates Environmental Learning. Thank you for sharing your wisdom.

I am also grateful to the Ontario Arts Council for their financial support.

Finally, two major events occurred while I was writing this book. The Asian tsunami and Hurricane Katrina will forever be reminders of the power of water. My thoughts continue to be with those whose lives have been affected by these disasters.

First published in the UK in 2007
by A&C Black Publishers Limited
38 Soho Square
London W1D 3HB
www.acblack.com

Text © 2007 Rochelle Strauss
Illustrations © 2007 Rosemary Woods

ISBN 978-0-7136-8761-3

Published in Canada by
Kids Can Press Ltd.
29 Birch Avenue
Toronto, ON M4V 1E2

www.kidscanpress.com

Published in the U.S. by
Kids Can Press Ltd.
2250 Military Road
Tonawanda, NY 14150

Edited by Val Wyatt
Designed by Marie Bartholomew
Printed and bound in Singapore

11 10 09 08 07
10 9 8 7 6 5 4 3 2 1

A&C Black uses paper produced with elemental chlorine-free pulp, harvested from managed sustainable forests. It is natural, renewable and recyclable. The logging and manufacturing processes conform to the environmental regulations of the country of origin.

One Well

Written by Rochelle Strauss

Illustrated by Rosemary Woods

A & C Black • London

One Well

Imagine for a moment that all the water on Earth came from just one well.

This isn't as strange as it sounds. All water on Earth *is* connected, so there really *is* just one source of water – one global well – from which we all draw our water. Every ocean wave, every lake, stream and underground river, every raindrop and snowflake and every chunk of ice in glaciers and polar ice caps is part of this global well.

So whether you are turning on a tap in the UK, pulling a bucket from a well in Kenya or swimming in a river in India, it is all the same water. Because it is all connected, how we treat the water in the well will affect every species on the planet, including humans, now and for years to come.

Do all planets have water?
Earth is the only planet in our solar system that has liquid water. This also means that it is the only planet that can support life.

Why is water so important?
You need water, and so does every other living organism — every person, every plant and every animal. Without water, nothing can survive.

Will Earth run out of water?
The amount of water on Earth will never change. It has been the same for billions of years.

The water in the well

We live on a watery planet. Almost 70 per cent of Earth's surface is covered with water. This surface water is found everywhere from oceans, lakes and rivers to streams, marshes, puddles and the morning dew. There is so much water that if you look down at Earth from space, it seems to be blue.

There is also water we can't see, beneath the Earth's surface. This 'groundwater' can be found just about everywhere. It fills the cracks in rocks underground. It fills the spaces between rocks, grains of sand and soil. Most groundwater is close to the Earth's surface, but some of it is buried quite deep. Water is also frozen in glaciers and polar ice caps. There is even water in the atmosphere, the layer of gases that surrounds Earth. Every one of these water sources feeds Earth's One Well.

Where is the water on Earth?

Oceans	97.23 per cent
Ice caps and glaciers	2.14 per cent
Groundwater	0.61 per cent
Freshwater lakes	0.009 per cent
Inland saltwater seas	0.008 per cent
Soil	0.005 per cent
Atmosphere	0.001 per cent
Rivers	0.0001 per cent

Yes, there is more water in the atmosphere and soil than in all of Earth's rivers!

Recycling water in the well

The water you drank today may have rained down on the Amazon rainforest five years ago. A hundred years ago, it may have been steam escaping from a teapot in India. Ten thousand years ago, it may have flowed in an underground river. A hundred thousand years ago, it may have been frozen solid in a glacier. And a hundred million years ago, it may have been a dinosaur's drink!

The amount of water on Earth doesn't change – there's no more water now than when the dinosaurs walked the Earth. The same water is just recycled over and over again. This constant movement of water from place to place is called the water cycle.

During the water cycle, water evaporates from oceans, lakes, rivers, ponds and puddles, and even from plants and animals. It rises into the air as water vapour.

As water vapour rises, it cools into tiny water droplets. This is called condensation. These droplets form clouds. Gradually, clouds collect more and more water droplets. The average white cloud weighs about twice as much as a blue whale.

When water droplets get too heavy, they fall from clouds as hail, snow or rain. These are called precipitation. Through precipitation, water returns to oceans, lakes and rivers. It also seeps into the soil and down into the groundwater. Year after year, water continuously circulates through the water cycle.

The water cycle

Are plants part of the water cycle?
In one year, an area of rainforest the size of a football pitch can pump over 75,000 litres of water vapour into the atmosphere – more than enough to fill a swimming pool.

How big is a raindrop?
It takes about one million tiny water droplets to make just one raindrop.

Why are oceans salty?
As rivers flow towards the sea, they collect salt from rocks and soil and add it to the ocean. As ocean water evaporates, the salt is left behind.

How thirsty is a tree?
On a summer's day,
an average-sized birch tree can
draw up about 300 litres of
water from the soil. That's
almost enough water to fill
two large baths.

**Which plant
uses the ocean to
spread its seeds?**
A coconut (the seed
of a palm tree) can
spend weeks, months
or even years drifting
in the ocean before
reaching land and
sprouting.

**How much
water is in plants?**
Tomatoes are about 95
per cent water. Apples are
about 85 per cent water.
Seeds are among the driest
foods – they contain only
5 to 10 per cent water.

Plants at the well

The first plants on Earth began life in the water. About 450 million years ago, some were washed ashore. At first they could live only in wet areas. Gradually they developed root systems that allowed them to tap into water in the soil.

Water is essential to plants. In fact, plants are mostly water. It's the water in their cells that gives plants their shape and form. Without it, they droop and shrivel.

All living things need food to survive. Water helps plants to make their own food. Plants use the sun's energy to change water and carbon dioxide into simple sugars. This process is called photosynthesis. Water then helps carry this food throughout the plant.

During photosynthesis, plants release water vapour into the air. Roots absorb water, which is carried to the stem. The stem acts like a water pipe in a house, letting water move up through the plant to the leaves. From the leaves, water is released back into the atmosphere. This is called transpiration. The transpired water is added to the cycle of water on Earth.

Plants are important to water, too. Roots anchor the soil they are buried in and stop it from blowing or washing into lakes and rivers.

Leaves and branches trap rain water, allowing it to seep slowly into the soil instead of flowing quickly away. And trees provide shade, which helps keep moisture in the soil.

Plants depend on water from the well for survival, and the well depends on plants to help move water through its cycle. Without plants, the water cycle would be disrupted. Without water, plants could not survive.

Animals at the well

Like plants, animals (including you) are mostly made of water. The water in animals is very important. It carries nutrients, helps digestion, removes waste, controls temperature, cleans eyes and keeps joints moving smoothly.

Water habitats are home to many of Earth's animals, and many more find their food in water. Watery species, such as fish, crabs, shrimp and zooplankton, are an important part of food chains around the world. A food chain is the link that connects animals (and other species), based on who eats whom. Without water-based species, food chains and food webs (collections of food chains) would collapse. Animals would starve.

Animals need water to survive, and they are also part of the water cycle. Animals add water to the atmosphere by breathing, sweating, weeing and even drooling. The water you brushed your teeth with today may have been the spray of a beluga whale ten years ago!

How much water is in animals?
Some of the 'wettest' animals on Earth are the jellyfish. They are about 95 per cent water. Frogs and earthworms are about 80 per cent water, while dogs, elephants and humans are about 70 per cent water.

Where do desert animals get water?
All animals need water to drink, even desert animals. They get much of the water they need from the food they eat.

Why do some animals live in water?
Animal life actually began in the ocean. About 360 million years ago, some animals started to evolve to find food and drink on land. Their bodies began to change and they slowly adapted to living on land.

What are saltwater marshes?
Saltwater marshes are wetlands that form where the land meets the sea. These habitats are home to a wide diversity of species, from tiny bacteria, fungi and algae to fish, crustaceans, reptiles, birds and mammals.

What are the smallest watery habitats?
Some rainforest frogs, insects, spiders, worms and bacteria live their entire lives in the tiny pools of water that get trapped by the leaves of the bromeliad plant.

Watery habitats

How can fish survive in frozen lakes?
Water freezes from the top down, and it rarely freezes right through to the bottom. The ice at the surface is like a blanket that stops the water below from freezing.

A habitat is a place where an animal can find everything it needs to live – food, shelter, space and water. Water is such an important part of an animal's habitat that if there isn't enough available, the animal will move away, even if all its other needs are met.

Most animals depend entirely on watery places, such as oceans, lakes and wetlands, for their habitat. Freshwater habitats (lakes, rivers, streams) are home to about 12 per cent of all the animal species in the world. Saltwater habitats (oceans, seas and some saltwater lakes) are home to 60 per cent of all fish species, as well as many other species, including some mammals and reptiles (such as whales, turtles and sea snakes).

Some of these animals live their whole lives in water and could not survive on land. Others, such as frogs, toads and many insects, spend part of their lives in the water and part on land.

Whether water is their habitat or just part of their habitat, animals could not survive without it.

What are coral reefs?
Coral reefs are found in the warm, shallow waters of oceans. They have been described as the rainforests of the sea because they are home to an incredible number of species.

People at the well

Since the beginning of time, people have depended on water – for drinking, food, bathing and watering crops. Water has always provided a route to move people and products from place to place. As societies grow, so does their need for water.

Today, water is essential in our homes, in industry and in agriculture. At home we use water for cleaning, cooking, drinking, flushing toilets and for bathing. But homes account for only 10 per cent of all the fresh water used.

About 21 per cent of the water used by humans goes to make everything from computers to cars. Water is an ingredient in many products, such as lotions, shampoos, chemicals and drinks. Water is used in hydroelectric power stations to generate electricity and in oil refineries to make petrol and diesel. In factories, water is used to heat things up or cool things down and to wash away waste. Water vapour (steam) has been used for hundreds of years to run machinery.

The remaining 69 per cent of the fresh water we use goes into agriculture. Farms use huge amounts of water to raise crops and livestock.

Look around – almost everything you see was made using water. It takes about 130 litres of water to make a bicycle. Water was used to grow the food you eat and make the clothes you wear. Water was even used to make the paper and ink for this book.

How much water does it take to produce a glass of milk?

About 185 litres, or 20 buckets! This includes the water the cow drinks, the water used to grow food for the cow and the water needed to process the milk in a dairy.

How much water does it take to produce a car?

About 147,000 litres of water is needed to make one family car.

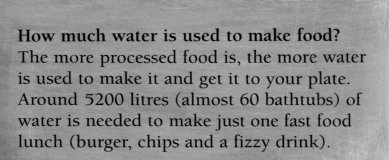

How much water is used to make food?

The more processed food is, the more water is used to make it and get it to your plate. Around 5200 litres (almost 60 bathtubs) of water is needed to make just one fast food lunch (burger, chips and a fizzy drink).

How much water do we use at home?

In UK homes, about three-quarters of all water is used in the bathroom. One flush of an average toilet uses nearly 13 litres.

Do humans depend on watery habitats to find their food?

Nearly a billion people around the world depend on fish as their main source of protein.

How much water do we need to drink?

People need an average of 2.5 litres of water a day, but much of this comes from food. In your lifetime, you will drink the equivalent of a swimming pool full of water.

Where is the world's deepest lake?
Lake Baikal in southeast Siberia contains almost one-fifth of all the fresh water on Earth. It's also home to the Baikal seal, one of the world's few freshwater seals.

How much of Earth's water is in the atmosphere?
Approximately 0.001 per cent! If a tanker truck represents all the water on Earth, the water in the atmosphere would barely fill a third of a fizzy drink can.

Why is so much water locked up in glaciers?
Because they are so big! The Bering Glacier in Alaska is the largest in North America. It's about five times bigger than New York City and nearly twice as tall as the Empire State Building.

Where does our drinking water come from?
More than half the drinking water used around the world comes from underground aquifers. These are layers of gravel, porous (holey) rocks or soil that trap large amounts of water.

Fresh water in the well

Though we live on a watery planet, not all of that water can be used to meet our needs. That's because humans and many other species depend on fresh water, and supplies of fresh water are limited.

Most of the water on Earth is salt water – almost 97 per cent. Only 3 per cent is fresh water. If a tanker truck filled with water represented all the water on Earth, then the planet's fresh water would fill a large bathtub.

But most of the fresh water – more than 99 per cent – is frozen in ice caps and glaciers, trapped deep underground or in the atmosphere, so we can't use it. How much fresh water is available to us? Remember that bathtub? Imagine filling nine fizzy drink cans from it. This represents all the fresh water we can use.

While there is a lot of water on the planet, we have access to less than 1 per cent of it.

Access to the well

Some families are lucky. They can turn on a tap to get drinking water, to fill a bathtub, to wash their car or to water the garden. But other families around the world are less fortunate. One billion people – almost 16 per cent of Earth's population – have to walk more than fifteen minutes to get to the nearest water supply.

There, they gather water for the day. Just a few jugs have to be used for drinking, cooking and cleaning. Other families don't have access to enough water to meet even these most basic needs.

While the amount of water on Earth is always the same, the *distribution* of water across the world isn't. Huge differences in rainfall can happen from country to country and even within the same country. Less rainfall means less water available in lakes, rivers and aquifers. Sometimes there just isn't enough water where it's needed most.

Because water is not evenly distributed across the globe, nearly one-fifth of the world's population does not have access to enough water. Many of these people live in Africa and Asia.

How does this affect children?
In many countries women and children have to collect water for the whole family. A bucket of water weighs 10 kg – try picking one up and imagine if you had to carry it for several kilometres every day. Children who are responsible for collecting water have little time left to go to school or play with friends.

Who uses the most water?
The average North American uses 400 litres of water every day.
North America has one-third of the population of Africa, yet
North Americans use three times as much water. How is this
possible? Nearly 300 million people in Africa do not have
access to enough fresh water.

Place
Average daily water use per person
1 bucket = 10 litres

Place	Average daily water use per person
North America	55 buckets
Richer European countries	27½ buckets
Poorer European countries	14 buckets
India	7 buckets
Nepal	3 buckets
Haiti	1½ buckets
Ethiopia	1 bucket

The crisis of water access is getting worse.
The world's population and
water use keep growing.
China and India
are now home to over
one-third of the world's
population, but they only
have access to one-tenth of
the world's fresh water.

What will happen if we keep on using water like this?
By 2025, many experts predict that one out of every four people will live in a country that is short of water. By 2050, 4 billion people may be living without enough clean water.

A growing population doesn't just mean more household water use. We'll also need more water for crops and livestock in order to feed more people.

Why does meat production use so much water?
Every day, all the world's livestock (cattle, sheep, pigs, goats, chickens etc) drink more than 160,000 large tanker trucks full of water.

Demands on the well

6,563,107,901 … give or take a few. That's how many people there are on Earth, and that number is growing every day. More people means a greater demand for water. But this growing population isn't the only thing putting a strain on our water supplies. The average person today uses about six times more water than a hundred years ago.

A growing population also means we need more space. As towns and cities grow to accommodate all these people, they gobble up land, which also affects nearby water. Houses, buildings and roads sometimes take the place of wetland habitats, which puts animal species at risk. They also change the way rain water, lakes and streams flow. Tarmac and concrete stop rain water from refilling underground water supplies.

There are more of us, and our demand for water at home, in industry and in agriculture has grown tremendously. But all the water we have now is all the water we ever will have. There is no more water now than there was 100 or 1000 or even 10,000 years ago. There will be no more 100 years from now, when the population may be closer to 10 billion.

We need to find a balance between our demand for water and the amount of water that's available to us.

Are dams a good way to trap rain water for people to use?
While dams make more water available, they also change the flow of rivers and damage habitats.

Pollution in the well

The water cycle helps keep Earth's water clean. As water evaporates, minerals, chemicals and dirt are left behind. The water vapour that rises into the atmosphere is relatively clean. When rain falls back to Earth, some of it is filtered through rocks and sand and is cleaned even more. Even plants play a role. As water travels through them, plants remove chemicals in the water. Then they transpire clean water back into the air.

But more and more waste from industry, agriculture and homes is getting into the water. Run-off from gardens, city streets and farms washes soil and chemicals (such as pesticides, fertilisers and detergents) into lakes, rivers, streams and ponds. Pollution in the atmosphere from cars and factories mixes with water vapour in the air. The rain that falls pollutes surface water and groundwater. Our actions may be overloading water's natural ability to clean itself.

As more water becomes polluted, there is less clean water available. Nearly 80 per cent of all diseases in the world are caused by unsafe water. Wildlife suffers, too. Water pollution threatens the health of many species and habitats around the planet.

Because of water's self-cleaning powers, the effects of pollution can be stopped and quite possibly reversed. But first we need to reduce the amount of pollution that gets into the water.

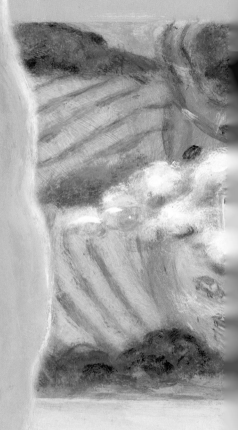

How many people don't have access to clean water?
A sixth of the world's population, or 1.1 billion people. Every year, 1.8 million children die from diseases caused by unclean water.

How else does water get polluted?
Every day, 1.8 million tonnes of rubbish are dumped into Earth's water. When human sewage gets into water it spreads viruses, bacteria and parasites.

Can't we just clean the water we use?
Dirty water from our houses is cleaned in sewage works before it joins the water cycle again. However, water treatment uses a huge amount of energy and are very expensive to build, expand and maintain.

What is acid rain?
Burning coal and other fuels in factories, power stations and vehicles pumps polluting gases into the air. These gases dissolve in water droplets in the atmosphere and make rain water more acidic than normal. Acid rain can fall thousands of kilometres from the source of the pollution, damaging and even killing wildlife.

25

Saving the water in the well

Water has the power to change everything. A single splash can make a seed sprout, quench thirst or provide a habitat. Water is the most basic and important need of all life on Earth. This gives it the power to unite – or divide – the world.

But Earth's One Well is in trouble. There is simply not enough clean water to go around.

Taking action to conserve water can help save the well. Conserving water means protecting both the quantity and quality of water on Earth. For example, using less water helps prevent water sources from drying up. Reducing water pollution protects the overall health of the well. Water conservation can help ensure there is enough clean water for everyone on the planet.

By becoming more aware of how you use water and by using less, you too can protect the water in Earth's One Well. Remember – every drop counts!

How can you help?

Water conservation isn't just something for governments, businesses and environmental groups to think about. Everyone needs to get involved in water conservation – even you. And it's not hard to do. It doesn't mean living without water. It just means becoming more aware of every splash of water you use.

Even the simplest actions can make a huge difference. For example, you could save water just by keeping a jug of drinking water in the fridge instead of letting the tap run to get cool water. By making sure you turn off taps so that they don't drip, you could save up to 10,000 litres (more than 100 bathtubs) of water a year.

Conserving water doesn't just mean using less water, it also means taking better care of the water we have. You can protect water from pollution by walking or cycling to school or to see friends instead of asking for a lift. This stops car exhaust gases from polluting water in the atmosphere. If you live near an ocean, lake, river or stream, you could organise beach or riverbank clean-ups to stop rubbish from getting into water. Planting trees anchors the soil so that it doesn't wash into waterways and make them muddy.

Imagine what would happen if each of us did just one thing to conserve water and protect Earth's One Well. These actions would add up. Together, they would help to ensure that there is enough clean water now and for years to come. Here are a few more ways you can help.

Learn more and teach others
By learning more about Earth's One Well, you can make choices everyday that help to conserve water. Then share what you learn. Help the people around you protect Earth's water too.

Join others to take action
There are many organisations working to protect water or to help people get the water they need. Find out more about organisations that interest you, and support their work by raising money, volunteering your time or helping to spread their message. Or start your own campaign.

Save water at home
With your family, list all the ways that you could reduce your water use at home. Some suggestions include:

- turning off the tap while washing your hands and brushing your teeth

- running dishwashers and washing machines only when full

- asking your parents to fix leaky taps

- collecting rain water or re-using bathwater to water the plants in your garden or house

- taking quick showers instead of baths.

Protect water
Rain water can wash waste and pollution into emergency drains, which flow into local rivers or lakes. Oil, grease, salt from roads, fertilisers and pesticides from gardens, paint, oil, leaves and litter can all end up in local waterways. Your school could start a campaign, such as painting fish symbols near sewers, to remind people that sewers empty into waterways, and encourage them to think before using chemicals in their homes and gardens.

Can a child make a difference?

You are never too young to start protecting Earth's water. Canadian schoolboy Ryan Hreljac is helping to make water more accessible to those who need it most. In 1998, as a six year old, Ryan learned that many people in Africa didn't have access to clean water. He decided to help, and raised enough money to build a well near a school in Uganda. But he didn't stop there. With his parents' help, he started the Ryan's Well Foundation, which continues to raise money to build wells in Africa and educate people elsewhere about the need to conserve water.

You can visit Ryan's website at www.ryanswell.ca/
Find more case studies and ideas at www.wateraid.org/uk
You'll find a list of everyday actions at www.waterwise.org.uk

Notes to parents, guardians and teachers

A crisis in the well

Throughout human history, we have relied heavily on water. It has influenced nearly every aspect of our lives. We've spent centuries learning how to harness water's incredible power and have become experts at catching and channelling it for our use. But our demand for water is growing rapidly and unsustainably. In our homes, we use six times more water now than we did a hundred years ago. Over the same period, the amount of irrigated land has more than doubled, greatly increasing water use. Industrial use has grown by almost four times since the 1950s alone.

And our growing consumption isn't the only problem. Other issues also threaten the health of Earth's One Well.

• Global warming and climate change affect weather and rainfall patterns around the world. As a result, some areas may experience extreme weather conditions and temperatures, which can lead to more flooding or drought. Over time, melting polar ice caps and warmer water may also cause sea levels to rise, altering the coastlines where many plants and animals live.

• Many of Earth's rivers cross international boundaries. But nations do not always work together to share this resource. Conflicts break out over who owns the water, how much is used and how it is used. How these fights are resolved will affect everyone.

• Habitats that surround the well are in crisis, too. Half of the world's wetlands have been drained. Dams have damaged habitats along 35 million km (22 million miles) of the world's rivers. And some of the most threatened species on Earth are those that depend on watery habitats.

• Water treatment plants are not always effective at keeping harmful substances from entering the water cycle. They can barely handle all the water they currently process, so how will they handle more as demand grows? Treatment plants also use a tremendous amount of energy. An increasing demand for treated water poses a serious threat to the health of the well. And expanding, replacing or fixing water treatment plants will be very costly.

Helping children become aware

As parents, teachers and guardians, we all have a role to play in helping our children understand the importance of water conservation. By fostering in them a sense of responsibility for Earth's One Well we can help children better understand the importance of all water on Earth and the issues facing the well. It will also encourage a sense of compassion and understanding for the needs of people around the world, as well as other species and habitats.

Most importantly, by working with our children to conserve and protect water – in our homes, schools, communities and local habitats – we show them not just how to live sustainably within the water cycle, but also how their actions can make a difference. Encouraging, supporting and guiding our children to become water aware will give them the confidence to make decisions and take action, now and in the future, that will protect Earth's One Well.

What can you do?
• **Get to know the issues**. Learn more about the crisis facing Earth's One Well and make changes in your day-to-day activities to conserve water.

• **Start a discussion** with your children about the value of water. Ask them to imagine what would happen if there was no water when they turned on a tap. What would it be like to live without toilets, baths or showers? To walk ten minutes, thirty minutes or even an hour to get water? How would they use water differently? What things might they do without? Remind them that every day many people around the world don't have enough water to meet their needs.

• **Celebrate World Water Day**, on 22 March each year. We are also in the United Nation's International Decade for Action – Water for Life (2005-2015). The goal of this decade is to promote greater awareness of water-related issues. Work with your children to promote water awareness at home, at school, in your community, and even in your city and county. Create water-oriented events, such as fetes, newsletters and invite speakers.

• **Encourage your family** or class to think critically about the water they use and the water they waste. Plan and implement water conservation initiatives at home and at school. In your garden, try planting drought-tolerant and/or native species, collecting rain water in a water butt and recycling partially dirty household 'grey' water. You could also install water meters and water-saving plumbing, such as low-flush toilets. As you implement these and other water-saving initiatives, talk to your children about what you are doing and why.

• **Adopt a waterway**. With your family or as a class, select a local water body (river, lake, wetland, etc.) and research its history. How has the water been used over the years? How has your city or town developed around it? Has the flow of water changed (or been changed)? What issues currently threaten it? Prepare a newsletter on your findings and circulate it throughout your school and community. Remind readers that we all need to work together to protect these local water systems.

We can no longer take it for granted that there will always be enough clean water for us, for our children or for our grandchildren. There is a crisis in the well and how we handle this crisis is one of the most important challenges facing the world today. Becoming water aware gives us all the power to protect Earth's One Well – and the potential to change the world.

Index